I0441454

HILLARY CLINTON
IN A "NUT" SHELL

ISBN-13: 978-1537000930

ISBN-10: 1537000934

Hillary Clinton, an icon among many women, many democrats, socialists, and communists, is as much a cult figure as Barack Obama was, but of a different color and gender. She's human, aging, and has a dream of being the first woman President of the United States. I don't blame her. She was the real President in the white house while her husband partied and signed documents. She had to forgive and forget his infidelities and live through his impeachment. She had to move to New York to find her niche among liberals and set her sights on the highest office in the world. She had to take orders from George Soros and step aside "for the greater good" to let Barack Obama make history before she did, legally or not.

She's been a woman trapped in the sixties as are so many of her peers, pretending to be working for the people while lining their own pockets and becoming more elite and privileged. I understand where she came from. Though I was raised a Republican, my vote, had I been of age, would have gone to John Kennedy. I was a Marine during the unpopular Viet Nam war, and though I proudly saluted my flag every day, I was also feeling the emotions of the anti-war movement. Actually, there are no people more against any war than those who serve us in the military and put their lives on the line.

When I finished my tour of duty, I went to work for a corporation, and also got involved in Women's Studies, totally unaware I was part of corporate America at the same time I was part of a Marxist-Feminist program. I didn't learn my lesson until I purchased a new car, for cash, and was promptly told I needed to loan that car to anyone and everyone because that was the socialist way. Like Hillary,

1

my "community" was my family, so I tried to follow their ideology. I loaned my car, got it back destroyed, and was told they hoped I had insurance. I wondered why they wouldn't share the cost of repair as I had to share the valuable asset that was mine. I didn't realize that they were the University elite, and I was, as Stalin said, the useless idiot.

So I get where Hillary comes from. The big difference is, I never lied or cheated or stole anything. I maintained my integrity, and most importantly, I remembered my roots and the roots of my ancestors. I remembered what the founders meant when they risked their lives and fortunes to forge documents that would constitute the greatest experiment and country in the world.

I've studied Hillary since Arkansas, through Whitewater, through her sudden fortunes in the market. I didn't vote for the Clintons, but I remember their rally song. I didn't want to stop thinking about tomorrow, but I wanted yesterday to be remembered and cherished. I studied her healthcare plan and knew it wasn't right for America. I watched her fail time and again and then use Bill's charm to fade away to the background. I watched her move to New York and set up housekeeping, nothing but a ploy to run for Senator. She used her gender and false celebrity to win, and I knew right then her next stop was back to the White House. She had been the woman behind the man and there was no way she was going to let history remember her that way.

As a student of Saul Alinsky's and a friend of George Soros, she got the financial backing to take on the presidential election. The problem was, she'd have to face the diversity that feminists and radicals were fighting for, and back down against a black man so as not to lose the election. I'm sure she was promised the Secretary of State position, not because she would be good at it, but because it would take her to all the countries she and Bill needed to amass their millions, give her the contacts she needed for the future, and secure enough data on leaders around the globe so any chance of stifling her mission would be met with the threat of blackmail, or worse.

Sure, Greenspan did a great job for Bill Clinton with the economy, even if the Federal Reserve was empty, but Bill's foreign policy and white house parties got the best of him, and also the best of her.

Her mistakes and false ideology during her tenure as Secretary of State have caused chaos throughout the Middle East. Her poor judgment on running guns through Libya to Syria cost 4 American lives, made the Clinton Foundation a lot of money, and is something she'll deny being responsible for until her death bed.

And now she again is running for President. Though there is much evidence that she won the nomination through fraud and deceit, she needed and wanted that moment when all saw her accept, the moment that many believe made history, and the adoration of many who believe she's capable just because she's a woman. Nancy Pelosi has said, "It doesn't matter what Hillary's record is, the important thing is she's a woman." How sad that the party who has tried to erase gender then relies on gender as the bargaining chip to stay blind to all the corruption it took to get there.

This book is short and to the point. Some things will be recognizable because they've made the news or the internet. Some things will seem incredible. Some things will hit home. Everything in this book can be referenced and documented through news outlets such as the Associated Press, ABC News and Reuters. Quotes and statements are on video and verifiable. Nothing in this book is conjured or conspiracy. Not everything is included as the list of denials, lies, and corruption are far too long for the average reader.

We are at a crossroads in our nation's history that can only be defined, as Ronald Reagan said, the choice between up or down for our nation. We are either the beacon of freedom, or the dimming light of communist subservience. We are either the greatest nation on earth, or we will be the greatest failure of a free people in history. We don't always the best people to vote for, and the division in modern American is great, but given the choice between Socialism, which is the last step to Communism, or the opportunity to once again be a nation that's strong, financially sound, and free, I only see one choice.

Hillary Rodham Clinton

1 – She's the first presidential spouse to ever be subpoenaed. This was specifically for her involvement on the Whitewater controversy. If it doesn't sound familiar, it's because this happened during husband Bill's presidential campaign and first years in office. As the facts stand: The New York Times printed an article alleging the Clintons invested and lost money in the Whitewater Development Corporation, a failed venture. From there, an investigation arose with Bill and Hillary as the focus, and

this led to a grand jury subpoena for both Clintons while Bill was still in office to turn over all related documents. 15 people ended up convicted of federal charges (though four of them got pardons from husband Bill right before he left office).

2 – She laughed while admitting she got child rapist off the hook. In 1975, Clinton, as an attorney, represented a man accused of raping a 12-year-old girl whose family he lived with. Having to defend her client to the best of her ability, she negotiated a plea deal that turned a potential 30-year sentence into one year and four years' probation. But the bad part doesn't involve the sentence—while being interviewed in the mid-1980s, Clinton acknowledged (but did not explicitly state) her client lied about raping a child and still passed a polygraph. "I had him take a polygraph, which he passed, which forever destroyed my faith in polygraphs

Usnews.com

3 – She made cash off pollution. As an attorney, Clinton made serious cash through her law firm and by being on corporate boards before she married husband Bill and took on her "good wife" image. Some of that cash—roughly $31,000 per year—came from Lafarge, a company later fined $1.8 million by the EPA for pollution in 1992 (a fine Clinton herself never had to pay despite her making money off the company). Funny enough, the Clinton administration ending up knocking that fine down to under $600,000. They do say it's all about who you know.

4 – She and Bill are the first and only couple to be fingerprinted by the FBI. This was due to a scandal during the Clinton administration: "Filegate." In 1996, the Clintons were believed to have improper access to FBI files. The White House's personnel security director improperly requested FBI reports including people who'd served in previous Republican administrations. And it was there that concern of a "dirty tricks" operation was in place by the Clintons—something Nixon had operated too. With that, Judiciary Committee chair, Orrin Hatch, requested the FBI perform fingerprint analyses on both Clintons. However, the FBI confirmed neither Clinton handled files personally—the beauty of having aides—though her fingerprints were found on relevant requested documents…two years later, in her family quarters.

5 – She associated with donors who wound up in jail. When Clinton ran for president in 2008, Norman Hsu, a big Democrat party contributor and fundraiser, was the man who collected contributions for the party, with these coming from a variety of "sources." He went long and far to promote Clinton, but it turned out Hsu was a criminal and—believe it or not—a fugitive who had been scamming people and businesses for years—$20 million worth. Also, years before that in mid-90s, Jorge Cabrera was a Democratic supporter who even wrote a personal check of $20,000 to the party. He was even seen in press pictures with Clinton as First Lady—a few months later, Cabrera was arrested in a Miami drug bust and got 19 years in prison. Again, it's all about who you know.

6 – She and her State Department failed to label Boko Harem a terrorist outfit. Despite the urging of many within Obama's administration and hard evidence, Secretary of State Clinton didn't label this Nigerian-based Islamic terrorist group a terror threat. Evidence was presented to the State Department in 2011, but Boko Haram remained off the terror list until 2013. One government watchdog group found evidence of political conflicts of interest involving foreign donations and the Clinton Foundation, but it is also interesting to note that Boko Haram didn't become a terrorist outfit until after Obama was reelected.

7 – She knew about Bill harassing Paula Jones and did nothing. Paula Jones was a government worker in Arkansas while husband Bill was governor there, and she alleged she was sexually harassed by Bill while he was there. She filed a suit in 1994, calling for just under $1 million in damages, though the case was settled out of court. Years later in 2015, the same Paula Jones told reporters she believed Hillary knew all about the harassment yet did nothing and simply supported her husband. Such accusations had weight behind it because of Juanita Broaddrick, a woman who claimed Bill raped her in 1978 and accused Hillary of "trying to silence her."

NBC News

8 – She and her State Department are the reason a US Ambassador was killed in Benghazi. With the deaths of four Americans, including sitting US Ambassador J. Christopher Stevens, during the attacks in Benghazi, Libya, the State Department initially described this incident as a spontaneous one when it was actually planned and premediated. Many suspect the State Department's desire for a low profile to be the reason why the compound's security was below standard—Clinton claimed responsibility for the lapses, but tried to abscond personal blame by pointing to other professionals in her department who handled security directly.

9 – She was the central figure behind Travelgate, the Clinton administration's first major ethics controversy. In this scandal, seven White House employees were fired from its Travel Office for "irregularities," some saying so friends of the Clintons could get on staff. Further evidence suggested Clinton orchestrated the firings and was believed to have lied under oath years before when the investigations started, as newly discovered evidence contradicted her statements that she'd had no involvement. Many, unsurprisingly, felt a cover-up was in place.

10 – She thinks women who accuse men of sexual harassment are "whiney." It's safe to say if Clinton were Republican, everyone would've heard about her characterization of women who dare to accuse men of sexually harassment, which anyone with sense would tell you is a genuine problem, as the "whiney women," aka victims, of former Senator Bob Packwood (R-OR) would likely agree. According to the notes of Clinton's good friend, late Professor Diane Blair, she was "tired of all those whiney women, and she needs [Bill] on health care." Because political priorities take precedence over sexual mistreatment and such—this coming from the woman who invokes the "war on women" to regularly push her agenda.

11 – She took money from Wal-Mart and never acknowledged it afterward. Between 1986 and 1992, Clinton was on the Wal-Mart board, which has been repeatedly criticized for supposed anti-union activity— Clinton, of course, did nothing about it on a board that included John Tate, who famously said, "Labor unions are

nothing but blood-sucking parasites living off the productive labor of people who work for a living." Clinton's 2008 campaign biography made absolutely no mention of Wal-Mart, and even further, Clinton was described as "loyal company woman" by Tate himself Since, you know, a paycheck is a paycheck, even when supreme lack of respect is running rampant.

12 – She called the Bill Clinton/Monica Lewinsky affair a "Vast Right Wing Conspiracy." This was her response to the rumors about husband Bill and then White House intern Monica Lewinsky: "The great story here for anybody willing to find it and write about it and explain it, is this vast right-wing conspiracy that has been conspiring against my husband since the day he announced for president." One can get the whole woman scorned fact of the matter, but this of course fell flat when Bill admitted to the affair after lying about it, becoming the second President to be served the Articles of Impeachment. Since then, Clinton's phrase has become part of the Democrat's toolkit, being used many times including to describe press attacks against Pres. Obama.

USA Magazine

13 – She claimed to have come under sniper fire in Bosnia before recanting. When Clinton was First Lady in 1996, she made an official visit to Bosnia to meet with American troops stationed there after the Bosnian War (started in response to the breakup of Yugoslavia) ended. After she returned, she told the press she and her then 16-year-old daughter came under sniper fire and could have been killed at the airport. One week later, Clinton took back her comments, claiming to have "made a mistake" in recounting what happened—especially given that news footage showed her calmly walking from her plane. She may have figured out claiming the First Lady and Daughter were under fire in a war-torn, unstable country was a bad idea if completely false.

14 – She and Bill took items from the White House that weren't theirs. When the Clintons moved out of White

House at the start of the Bush administration, there were allegations of "damage, theft, vandalism, and pranks" in abundance. From there, upon moving into their New York home after the White House, they brought along a whopping $190,000 worth of items that should have been left in their place, considering those items actually did not belong to either Clinton. Clinton and husband Bill did ultimately return the items, but the fact that it happened at all is interesting when considering Clinton's own admission that she and her husband were broke and in debt when they left the White House.

15 – She gave speeches for $225,000 a piece but banned the press from them. All three Clintons—Hillary, Bill, and Chelsea—have earned income through speeches. One year, Clinton made $11 million for 51 speeches, averaging around $225,000 each. With the level of leverage that she has, Clinton could have even gotten away with a greater fee, especially given her speeches were for Goldman Sachs and other Wall Street bigwigs. More than that, however, Clinton clouds these speeches in complete privacy to the point no one really knows what she talks about, promoting a secrecy akin to that of the Free Masons. No media, press, live tweeting, or photos, leaving many suspicious of her coziness with big money, many like that guy Bernie Sanders. One reporter claims to have never seen so much secrecy for such a big event—because that's just how she rolls apparently with her opaque self.

16 – She endangered national security to have a private email server. During Clinton's time as Secretary of State,

she exclusively used a private email server rather than the official State Department's federal servers—the kind that are designed to the best of their ability to protect classified information including the names of operatives overseas and in the US. By asserting control of her server, Clinton and her sides could decide which emails to turn over to the State Department when requested and which emails not to—as such, the State Department has actually "lost" digital copies of many of the emails the FBI has requested, calling it a "clerical" error. Given that "CIA names just fall off the page" of Clinton's easily hackable emails, if she doesn't face indictment at the end of the FBI's investigation, it will be a colossal joke.

17 – And finally: She claims to have communed with Eleanor Roosevelt. Bob Woodward reported that while in the White House, Clinton used to have "chats" with long dead First Lady Eleanor Roosevelt and even Gandhi (also long dead). Such conversations were facilitated by Jean Houston, co-director of the Foundation for Mind Research, who actually moved into the White House for a spell—when asked by Houston if she would ever want to address Jesus, Clinton said it would be "too personal." Admittedly, this is less a scandal and more just something weird as hell, but this story alone represents the major power of left-wing media bias. No one has heard of this, but everyone knew about Nancy Reagan and her love for astrology to the point of ridiculous contention.

THE WORST LIES

Dead Broke – In an interview, Clinton stated that she "came out of the White House not only dead broke, but in debt." Something even the left-leaning Politifact found to be false.

Sniper Fire – During the 2008 campaign, Clinton said she came under sniper fire in Bosnia during the '90s. She went so far as to claim her group ran "with our heads down to get into the vehicles to get to our base." Video of her actual arrival surfaced showing a very calm scene instead, and the Democrat would quickly say she simply misspoke.

Immigrant Grandparents – When discussing immigrant stories, Clinton asserted that "all my grandparents… came over here." It was another story Politifact said was false, as only one of her grandparents was an immigrant.

Sir Edmund Hillary – Seems Clinton can't even bring herself to tell the truth about her own name. She claimed to be named after Sir Edmund Hillary, one of the first men to climb Mt. Everest. One small problem though, the explorer didn't climb Everest until Clinton was 6 years old.

The Few, The Proud, The Marines – Very recently, Clinton claimed to have been turned down by the Marines when she applied in 1975. Washington Post fact-checkers quickly realized the absurdity that a rising legal star at the time, and soon to be wife of Bill Clinton, would drop everything and ship off with the Marines. They gave her a couple of Pinocchios for her tall tale.

Secret E-Mails – Former Secretary of State Clinton claimed her infamous private e-mail server was set up in "accordance with the rules and the regulations in effect." A federal judge disagreed, saying Clinton "violated government policy" when she used a private server to store official State Department messages.

Benghazi – Clearly the most reprehensible lie of them all – Clinton failed to tell the truth about a terrorist attack that killed four Americans in Benghazi. She claimed for weeks, standing over the flag-draped coffins of murdered Americans, that an insensitive YouTube video had incited the violence that occurred that night. Why? Because a terrorist attack on the anniversary of 9/11 – which it was – would have destroyed President Obama's re-election chances.

BODIES AND QUOTES

What Hillary says and what she actually does are almost always two entirely different things, but the most curious thing that happens with Hillary and Bill is if you disagree with them or threaten to "tell" on them, you might very well disappear.

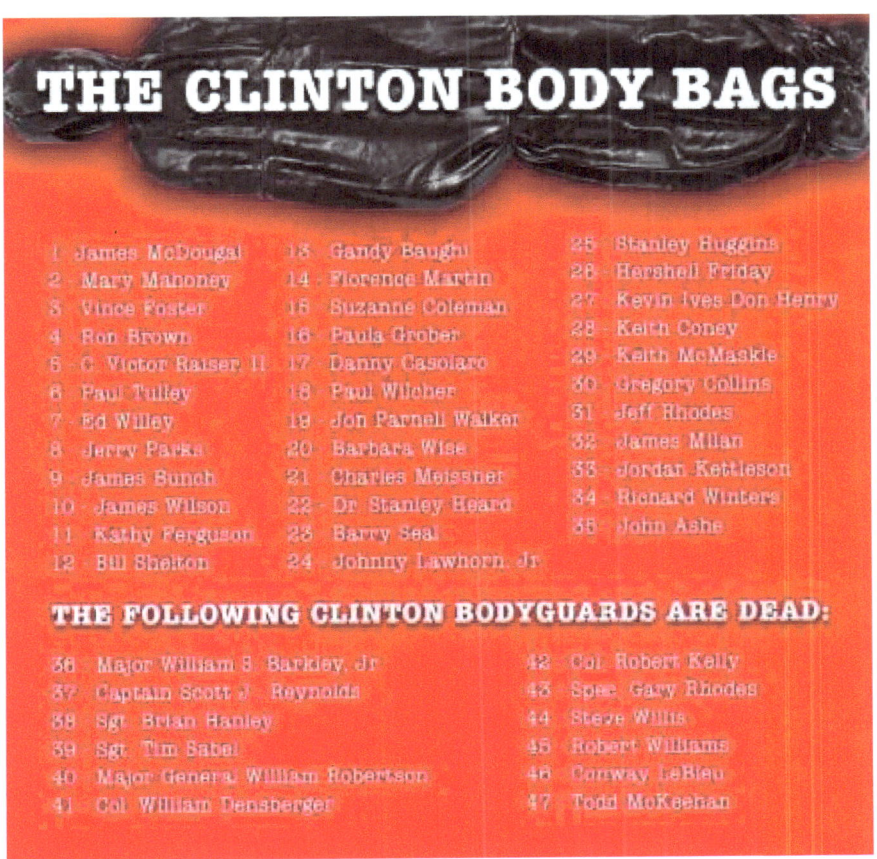

Arlinreport.com

The back story on these associates of the Clintons is far too long for this publication, but the most notable for those who want to do the research are **Vince Foster,** one of the first alleged suicides, and **John Ashe**, former United Nations General Assembly President.

Dailymail.com

Died: June 22, 2016

Initially reported as having died from a heart attack, John's throat had obviously been crushed. At that point the official story changed to him accidentally dropping a barbell on his own throat (the plotline from the episode "An Exercise in Fatality" from the TV series "Columbo.") crushing his larynx.

Ashe was about to begin trial for a bribery charge involving Chinese businessman Ng Lap Seng, who had been implicated but not charged in the 1996 "China-gate" scandal for funneling illegal donations to Bill Clinton's re-election fund through Arkansas restaurant owner Charlie Trie. Ashe was supposed to testify about Hillary's links to Ng Lap Seng.

Hillary's direct quotes, some of which those without able or internet never heard, give you an idea of where she really stands on almost any issue.

1) "Many of you are well enough off that the tax cuts may have helped you. We're saying that for America to get back on track, we're probably going to cut that short and not give it to you. We're going to take things away from you on behalf of the common good." – Hillary Clinton

Translation: A tax increase of $1.3 trillion dollars and spending that will be called investments.

2) "Don't let anybody tell you that it's corporations and businesses that create jobs." -- Hillary Clinton

Translation: Undocumented workers and the government create jobs.

3) "You know, we can't keep talking about our dependence on foreign oil and the need to deal with global warming and the challenge that it poses to our climate and to God's creation and just let business as usual go on, and that means something has to be taken away from some people." – Hillary Clinton

Translation: Coal and Oil, fossil fuel jobs, need to be destroyed.

4) "I can't worry about every undercapitalized business" — Hillary Clinton testifying before Congress on the effects of Nationalized Health Care.

Translation: Small businesses will suffer the most under Hillarycare/Obamacare.

5) "Yes, we've cut the maternal mortality rate in half, but far too many women are still denied critical access to reproductive health care and safe childbirth, and laws don't count for much if they're not enforced. Rights have to exist in practice — not just on paper. Laws have to be backed up with resources and political will. **And deep-seated cultural codes, religious beliefs and structural biases have to be changed."** – Hillary Clinton.

Translation: Catholics, Christians have to change their beliefs about abortion.

6) "We are at a stage in history in which remolding society is one of the great challenges facing all of us in the West." -- Hillary Clinton per Barbara Olson's Hell to Pay: The Unfolding Story of Hillary Rodham Clinton.

Translation: Cultural engineering. from the Fabian Socialists, which includes genocide, abortion and the infiltration of Islam.

7) "There are rich people everywhere. And yet they do not contribute to the growth of their own countries.....They don't invest in public schools, in public hospitals, in other kinds of development internally." – Hillary Clinton.

Translation: We need to tax the rich as much as possible and continue foreign aid from American tax dollars to other countries, like rich Saudi Arabia.

8) "No. We just can't trust the American people to make those types of choices ... Government has to make those choices for people." – Hillary Clinton.

Translation: Democrats believe people are not smart enough, educated enough, to understand what needs to be done to make the changes they want to make. Government will decide for the people.

9) "If you have guns in your home, tell your parents to keep them away from you and your friends and your little brothers and sisters." -- Hillary Clinton to middle school students.

Translation: The second amendment of the Constitution needs to be revised, eliminated so the government can have control of guns.

10) "I also believe that every new handgun sale or transfer should be registered in a national registry..." -- Hillary Clinton.

Translation: Gun control, disarming Americans.

11) "I think again we're way out of balance. We've got to rein in what has become almost an article of faith that almost anybody can have a gun anywhere at any time. And I don't believe that is in the best interest of the vast majority of people." -- Hillary Clinton.

Translation: Though there are more than 93 million gun owners in America, and gun deaths are caused by illegal weapons, the government needs to keep guns from Americans.

12) "We came out of the White House not only dead-broke, but in debt. We had no money when we got

there and we struggled to piece together the resources for mortgages, for houses, for Chelsea's education. It was not easy." – Hillary Clinton (In less than 7 years, the Clinton's net worth is over $200 million dollars.)

Translation: So the Clintons formed the Clinton Global Initiative, a money laundering organization set up for their personal benefit.

13) "I remember landing under sniper fire. There was supposed to be some kind of a greeting ceremony at the airport, but instead we just ran with our heads down to get into the vehicles to get to our base." — Hillary Clinton makes up a ridiculous, untrue story about her trip to Bosnia.

Translation: Either confusion from her mental illness, or the desire to be a hero and garner the sympathy vote.

14) "In the four years since the inspectors left, intelligence reports show that Saddam Hussein has worked to rebuild his chemical and biological weapons stock, his missile delivery capability, and his nuclear program. He has also given aid, comfort, and sanctuary to terrorists, including Al Qaeda members, though there is apparently no evidence of his involvement in the terrible events of September 11, 2001. It is clear, however, that if left unchecked, Saddam Hussein will continue to increase his capacity to wage biological and chemical warfare, and will keep trying to develop nuclear weapons.

Should he succeed in that endeavor, he could alter the political and security landscape of the Middle East, which as we know all too well affects American security." — Hillary Clinton, October 10, 2002

Translation: Vote to invade Iraq. She would later tell America we should look at the war in Iraq as a business opportunity. As the candidate for President, she now says she was against the Iraq war.

15) "There's a different leader in Syria now. Many of the members of Congress of both parties who have gone to Syria in recent months have said they believe he's a reformer." -- Hillary Clinton on tyrannical maniac Bashar Assad

Translation: We'll send weapons to Syria through Libya.

15) "With all due respect, the fact is we had four dead Americans. Was it because of a protest or was it because of guys out for a walk one night decided to go kill some Americans? What difference, at this point, does it make?" -- Hillary Clinton.

Translation: Ambassador Stevens knew about the weapon sales to Syria that were forming what we know as ISIS. He needed to die "for the greater good."

16) "My husband may have his faults, but he has never lied to me." -- Hillary Clinton per Kim Eisler's Masters of the Game: Inside the World's Most Powerful Law Firm.

Translation: Bill Clinton only lies under penalty of perjury and under oath.

17) "Put this (helicopter) on the ground! I left my sunglasses in the limo. I need those sunglasses. We need to go back!" -- Hillary Clinton from Air Force Lt. Colonel Robert Patterson's Dereliction of Duty.

Translation: Secret Service and military personnel state that Hillary has a vile temper and personality and blatant disrespect for the Military, Police and anyone in authority.

18) "I have to admit that a good deal of what my husband and I have learned (about Islam) has come from my daughter. (As) some of you who are our friends know, she took a course last year in Islamic history." – Hillary Clinton.

Translation: As Secretary of State, she was so busy granting favors and being bought, that she learned what she thought she needed to know about Islam from college course.

19) "The last time I actually drove a car myself was 1996." -- Hillary Clinton.

Translation: As one of the global elites, Hillary is not only above the law, but totally out of touch with the American reality.

Hillary's flip flops are also essential reading. Some may say she's evolved since the year 2000, but her quotes and speeches clearly point to changes in policy, and most likely, saying what voter's want to hear versus what she believes and will do.

Examples: She supported clean coal and now wants to put the coal industry out of business. She was against gay marriage, but is now for it. She opposed driver's licenses for illegals, but now is for it. She favored the Keystone XL pipeline while Secretary of State and now opposes it.

In 2006, She supported her husband's legislation on NAFTA, but in 2007, was against it as she readied her run for the presidency. In 2016, she is now for NAFTA and CAFTA and the Trans Pacific Trade agreement {TPP) that relinquishes American Sovereignty, but tells voters she against TPP because it's not popular with mos of the electorate.

Dailymail.com

Hillary vs. Hillary

THE TOP 22 RECENT CLINTON FLIP FLOPS

TRANS-PACIFIC PARTNERSHIP (TPP)
2012 Supports TPP | 2015 Opposes TPP

U.S.-KOREA FREE TRADE AGREEMENT (KORUS)
2012 Supports KORUS | 2015 Opposes KORUS

NORTH AMERICAN FREE TRADE AGREEMENT (NAFTA)
2006 NAFTA Good for Economy | 2007 NAFTA Bad for American Workers

COLOMBIA FREE TRADE AGREEMENT
2008 Opposes Agreement | 2011 Supports Agreement

CENTRAL AMERICAN FREE TRADE AGREEMENT (CAFTA-DR)
2005 Opposes CAFTA | 2015 Touts CAFTA

RAISING THE U.S. DEBT LIMIT
2006 Votes Against Raising Debt Limit | 2011 Increasing Debt Limit "Common-Sense"

RAISING PAYROLL TAXES
2008 Flatly Rejected | 2015 Suggests Increasing Limit

ARMING SYRIAN REBELS
2012 Expressed Doubt & Concern | 2014 Advocates Arming Rebels

SYRIA'S BASHAR AL ASSAD'S "REFORMER" CREDENTIALS
2011 Assad a "Reformer" | 2015 Claims Viewed As "Principal Threat"

U.S. EMBARGO ON CUBA
2000 Opposes Lifting Sanctions | 2015 Supports Lifting Embargo

IRAN'S RIGHT TO ENRICH URANIUM
2014 No Right to Enrichment | 2015 Supports Iran Deal, Allows Enrichment

KEYSTONE XL PIPELINE
2010 Favors Keystone XL | 2015 Opposes Keystone XL

ETHANOL MANDATE
2002 Opposes Ethanol Mandate | 2014 "Energy" Supports Ethanol Mandate

DEPORTATION OF ILLEGAL IMMIGRANTS WORKING IN THE U.S.
2003 Stop Employing Illegal Immigrants | 2015 Expand Obama's Executive Action

DRIVER'S LICENSES FOR ILLEGAL IMMIGRANTS
2008 Opposes Driver's Licenses | 2015 Supports Driver's Licenses

SANCTUARY CITIES
2007 Cities Can Ignore Federal Agencies | 2015 Cities Should Listen to Federal Requests

NEW FEDERAL GUN CONTROL
2008 Opposes "Blanket Rules" On Guns | 2015 Supports Stricter Gun Laws

GUN OWNERSHIP
2008 Attacked Obama on Gun Control | 2015 Gun Culture "Way Out of Balance"

GAY MARRIAGE
2008 Opposes Gay Marriage | 2013 Supports Gay Marriage

DEFENSE OF MARRIAGE ACT (DOMA)
2000 Supports DOMA | 2007 Repudiated Support for DOMA

CHARTER SCHOOLS
2013 Long-time Proponent of Charter Schools | 2015 Criticizes Charter Schools

CLEAN COAL
2008 Supports "Clean Coal" | 2012 Supports Strict Regulations on Coal

HILLARY'S HEALTH

1. Coughing fits — In February 2016, presidential candidate Clinton suffered her third public coughing fit during a speech in Harlem. "Clinton had to dig out a lozenge at last year's Benghazi hearings," noted the **Daily Mail**, and "also suffered a coughing fit in Iowa back in January, something she attributed to speaking a lot on her campaign tour." The fits prompted many to speculate as to what could be causing them. Ear, nose, and throat specialist Dr. Jonathan Aviv told **Inside Edition**, "It's not just cough. There's some hoarseness, there's some throat clearing, in fact there's frequent throat clearing. When you have these trio of symptoms, you have to think of what I call throat burn reflux, which is acid reflux affecting the throat."

2. Health attack on Sanders backfires — "Democratic presidential hopeful Bernie Sanders' campaign fundraised off a report that an ally of rival Hillary Clinton planned to demand Sanders release his medical records," **The Hill** reported in January. John Podesta, chairman of Clinton's campaign, tried to downplay the incident in an effort to draw attention away from Clinton's health. "We're fighting on who would make a better president, not on who has a better Physical Fitness Test," he tweeted.

3. Fall fractures elbow — While serving as President Barack Obama's secretary of state in mid-2009, Hillary Clinton fell and fractured her right elbow while walking to

her car in the basement of the State Department, **The New York Times** reported. Clinton, 61 at the time, underwent surgery to repair the elbow, and missed at least one meeting with Obama as a result. "Having broken my right arm as secretary of defense, and had the left arm operated on, I think I can truthfully say, I feel her pain," said Defense Secretary Robert M. Gates at the time. Secretary Clinton fell again in 2011 while boarding a plane to Oman, but did not sustain injury.

4. Faint causes concussion — In late 2012, Secretary Clinton "sustained a concussion after fainting," The **Associated Press** reported. The incident came just days before her scheduled testimony about the Sept. 11 attack against a U.S. diplomatic outpost in Benghazi, Libya, before the Senate Foreign Relations Committee. Other officials from the department attended in her stead. The State Department said Clinton was dehydrated because of a stomach virus, which had recently caused her to back out of a trip to North Africa and the Persian Gulf.

5. Blood clot — Secretary Clinton was hospitalized in December 2012 after doctors discovered a blood clot during a follow-up exam related to her concussion. "Mrs. Clinton's blood clot formed in a large vein along the side of her head, behind her right ear, between the brain and the skull," **The New York Times** reported, noting that Clinton also had a blood clot in her leg in 1998. She began taking blood thinners around the time of her hospital discharge. The concussion and subsequently discovered blood clot

forced Clinton to ultimately take a month-long absence from her role as secretary of state.

6. Prism glasses for double vision — "As she testified about the Sept. 11 attack on the U.S. Consulate in Libya, the secretary of state appeared to have tiny vertical lines etched onto the left lens of her new brown specs," the **New York Daily News** wrote in January 2013. "Clinton's spokesman confirmed Thursday night she is wearing the special glasses as a result of the fall and concussion she suffered last month, but he did not elaborate. Experts told the **Daily News** that Clinton likely has a Fresnel prism placed on her glasses. The adhesive panel is used to treat double vision." Fresnel prisms can be ground into a lens for longer term use, and the prism is not visible when built into the lens itself.

7. Prescription blood thinner — In August 2015, **The Associated Press** reported that Clinton was still taking Coumadin, a blood thinner used to prevent blood clots. "Her Coumadin dose is monitored regularly and she has experienced no side-effects from her medications," wrote Dr. Lisa Bardack, an internist who practices near Clinton's suburban New York home. Previously, in a 2014 interview with ABC's Diane Sawyer, Clinton said she was "probably" on blood thinners for life.

8. Thyroid — Along with her blood thinner, Clinton takes Armour Thyroid, a thyroid hormone replacement, antihistamines, and vitamin B12, the **AP** reported.

9. Brain damage comment — In May 2014, The **Washington Post** reported that Republican strategist Karl Rove "distanced himself from a provocative report in the **New York Post**, saying he does not believe — as the newspaper asserted he had said — that Clinton suffered 'brain damage' when she fell and sustained a head injury in December 2012." Rove had been commenting on Clinton's prism glasses.

10. Bill says recovery took six months — **Fox News** reported in May of 2014 that "Bill Clinton said earlier this week there's 'nothing to' the [Hillary] health questions — though at the same time, he revealed her recovery took about six months, which is much longer than the State Department had indicated."

Hillary Clinton's health records have still not been released, though computer hacked documents show that her concussion was far more serious than reported. She has been seen "freezing" when speaking to constiuents, "short circuiting" when speaking to reporters, and displas symptoms of seizure in videos.

Newsmax.com

HILLARY'S ACCOMPLISHMENTS

From the HillaryClinton.com website

1. Fought for children and families for 40 years and counting. After law school, Hillary could have gone to work for a prestigious law firm, but took a job at the Children's Defense Fund. She worked with teenagers incarcerated in adult prisons in South Carolina and families with disabled children in Massachusetts. It sparked a lifelong passion for helping children live up to their potential.

EXCEPT: The unborn have no constitutional rights and she is supported by Planned Parenthood for her stance on abortion rights.

2. Helped provide millions of children with health care. As first lady of the United States, Hillary fought to help pass health care reform. When that effort failed, she didn't give up: Hillary worked with Republicans and Democrats to help create the Children's Health Insurance Program. CHIP cut the uninsured rate of American children by half, and today it provides health care to more than 8 million kids.

EXCEPT:

The Clinton White House, while supportive of the idea of expanding children's health, fought the first SCHIP effort, spearheaded by Senators Edward M. Kennedy, Democrat of Massachusetts, and Orrin G. Hatch, Republican of Utah, because of fears that it would derail a bigger budget bill.

34

And several current and former lawmakers and staff said Hillary Clinton had no role in helping to write the congressional legislation, which grew out of a similar program approved in Massachusetts in 1996. "The White House wasn't for it. We really roughed them up" in trying to get it approved over the Clinton administration's objections, Hatch said in an interview. "She may have done some advocacy [privately] over at the White House, but I'm not aware of it."

3. Helped get 9/11 first responders the health care they needed. When terrorists attacked just months after Hillary became U.S. senator from New York, she worked to make sure the 9/11 first responders who suffered lasting health effects from their time at Ground Zero got the care they needed.

EXCEPT:

The actual 9/11 bill passed long after Clinton left the Senate: After the Senate vote, a celebration broke out in a room in the Capitol that was packed with emergency workers and 9/11 families, as well as the two senators from New York, Charles E. Schumer and Kirsten E. Gillibrand, and the two senators from New Jersey, Frank R. Lautenberg and Robert Menendez. The senators, all Democrats, were greeted with a huge ovation and repeated chants of "U.S.A.! U.S.A.!" Mr. Schumer, the state's senior senator, allowed Ms. Gillibrand to address the group first, in apparent deference to the role she took in the Senate on the 9/11 legislation. She started the job. Someone else finished.

4. Told the world that "women's rights are human rights." Standing in front of a U.N. conference and declaring that

"women's rights are human rights" was more controversial than it sounds today. Many within the U.S. government didn't want Hillary to go to Beijing. Others wanted her to pick a less polarizing topic (you say polarizing, we say half the population). But Hillary was determined to speak out about human rights abuses, and her message became a rallying cry for a generation.

EXCEPT:

Not a Kennedy speech or a Reagan speech, but this:

Women's Rights Women's reproductive rights and access to reproductive health remain severely curtailed under China's population planning regulations. That policy includes the use of legal and other coercive measures, such as administrative sanctions, fines, and coercive measures, including forced insertion of intrauterine devices and forced abortion, to control reproductive choices . . . China was reviewed under the Convention on the Elimination of All Forms of Discrimination against Women (CEDAW) in October. The committee expressed concerns over the lack of judicial independence and access to justice for women and retaliation against women rights activists. Chinese authorities prevented two activists from participating in the review: Ye Haiyan, China's most prominent sex worker rights activist, was placed under administrative detention, while HIV-AIDS activist Wang Qiuyun's passport was confiscated.

5. Stood up for LGBT rights at home and abroad. As secretary of state, Hillary made LGBT rights a focus of U.S. foreign policy. She lobbied for the first-ever U.N. Human Rights Council resolution on human rights and

declared that "gay rights are human rights." And here at home, she made the State Department a better, fairer place for LGBT employees to work.

EXCEPT:

As the State Senator of New York, she clearly stated she was against gay marriage.

As Secretary of State and with the Clinton Foundation, she received millions of dollars of donations from countries who brutalize and murder LGBT people.

CLINTON CORRUPTION

$6 billion went missing at the State Department during Clinton's tenure, according to a report from the Inspector General

From **The Fiscal Times**:

The State Department has no idea what happened to $6 billion used to pay its contractors.

In a special "management alert,", the State Department's Inspector General Steve Linick warned "significant financial risk and a lack of internal control at the department has led to billions of unaccounted dollars over the last six years.

The lack of oversight "exposes the department to significant financial risk," the auditor said. "It creates conditions conducive to fraud, as corrupt individuals may attempt to conceal evidence of illicit behavior by omitting key documents from the contract file. It impairs the ability of the Department to take effective and timely action to protect its interests, and, in turn, those of taxpayers."

In the memo, the IG detailed "repeated examples of poor contract file administration." For instance, a recent investigation of the closeout process for contracts supporting the mission in Iraq, showed that auditors couldn't find 33 of the 115 contract files totaling about $2.1 billion. Of the remaining 82 files, auditors said 48 contained insufficient documents required by federal law.

In another instance, the Bureau of International Narcotics and Law Enforcement issued a $1 billion contract in Afghanistan that was deemed "incomplete."

2. Clinton accepted millions of dollars from foreign governments while at the State Department in violation of ethics agreement with White House

From the **Washington Post:**

The Clinton Foundation accepted millions of dollars from seven foreign governments during Hillary Rodham Clinton's tenure as secretary of state, including one donation that violated its ethics agreement with the Obama administration, foundation officials disclosed Wednesday.

Most of the contributions were possible because of exceptions written into the foundation's 2008 agreement, which included limits on foreign-government donations.

The agreement, reached before Clinton's nomination amid concerns that countries could use foundation donations to gain favor with a Clinton-led State Department, allowed governments that had previously donated money to continue making contributions at similar levels ...

Some of the donations came from countries with complicated diplomatic, military and financial relationships with the U.S. government, including Kuwait, Qatar and Oman.

Other nations that donated included Australia, Norway and the Dominican Republic.

The donation from Qatar came while the country was vying for the World Cup, and was accompanied with a donation from FIFA (which everyone knows has a reputation for being totally above-board). Again, the Washington Post:

Former President Bill Clinton served as the honorary chairman of the U.S. committee that worked unsuccessfully to win the right to host the 2022 World Cup. The surprise winner that year was Qatar—and it turns out that the Qatari committee now planning the massive event has been a major donor to Clinton's charitable foundation.

The soccer-related donations to the Bill, Hillary and Chelsea Clinton Foundation came into focus Wednesday as U.S. Attorney General Loretta Lynch alleged deep rooted corruption at FIFA, the world's soccer governing organization. Also Wednesday, the Swiss announced a criminal investigation into Qatar's 2022 bid. The Clinton Foundation has no involvement with the investigations.

The foundation's donor records, posted on its Web site, show that FIFA, or the Fédération Internationale de Football Association, has donated between $50,000 and $100,000 to the Clinton foundation. The Qatar 2022 Supreme Committee, which was formed in 2011 to build stadiums and other infrastructure after Qatar was named the 2022 host, has given between $250,000 and $500,000 to the foundation.

3. Firms that paid millions in speaking fees to Clinton were also lobbying for government contracts while she was at the State Department

Trump and Sanders both criticized Clinton for the millions of dollars she made in speaking fees before financial services firms (and for her refusal to provide transcripts of those speeches). In reality, a wide variety of lobbying firms and government contractors were privately paying the Clintons.

From the **Associated Press:**

It's not just Wall Street banks. Most companies and groups that paid Democratic presidential candidate Hillary Clinton to speak between 2013 and 2015 have lobbied federal agencies in recent years, and more than one-third are government contractors, an Associated Press review has found. Their interests are sprawling and would follow Clinton to the White House should she win election this fall.

The AP's review of federal records, regulatory filings and correspondence showed that almost all the 82 corporations, trade associations and other groups that paid for or sponsored Clinton's speeches have actively sought to sway the government—lobbying, bidding for contracts, commenting on federal policy and in some cases contacting State Department officials or Clinton herself during her tenure as secretary of state.

Presidents are not generally bound by many of the ethics and conflict-of-interest regulations that apply to non-elected executive branch officials, although they are subject to laws covering related conduct, such as bribery and illegal gratuities. Clinton's 94 paid appearances over two years on the speech circuit leave her open to scrutiny over decisions she would make in the White House or influence that may affect the interests of her speech sponsors ...

The AP review identified at least 60 firms and organizations that sponsored Clinton's speeches and lobbied the U.S. government at some point since the start of the Obama administration. Over the same period, at least 30 also profited from government contracts. Twenty-two groups lobbied the State Department during Clinton's tenure as secretary of state. They include familiar Wall Street financial houses such as Morgan Stanley and Goldman Sachs Group Inc., corporate giants like General Electric Co. and Verizon Communications Inc., and lesser-known entities such as the Institute of Scrap Recycling Industries and the Global Business Travel Association …

Despite months of controversy over her speeches to Wall Street patrons, Clinton's biggest rewards came from Washington's trade associations, the lobbying groups that push aggressively for industry interests. Trade groups paid Clinton more than $7.1 million, the review showed.

The National Association of Realtors spent $38.5 million on government contacts in 2013, the same year it paid Clinton $225,000 to appear at the group's gathering in San Francisco. A group spokesman said Clinton was among former U.S. officials invited to share their experiences but said she was not paid as part of its lobbying activities.

The Biotechnology Industry Organization, which represents biotech and pharmaceutical firms, spent between $7 million and $8.5 million annually on lobbying since 2008, including contacts with the State Department—during Clinton's tenure—on the agency's biotech discussions with foreign governments. The trade group, which hosted Clinton for $335,000 at its event in San Diego in June 2014, has won more than $425,000 in federal payments since 2008 in work for the National Science Foundation and other agencies. The group did not respond to phone calls or emails for comment from AP.

The financial services and investment industry accounted for about $4.1 million of Clinton's earnings. Its ranks included not only Wall Street powerhouses like Morgan

Stanley, Goldman Sachs and Bank of America Corp., but also private equity and hedge funds like Kohlberg Kravis Roberts & Co. LP and Apollo Global Management LLC and foreign-owned banks such as Deutsche Bank AG and the Canada Imperial Bank of Commerce. Goldman Sachs, which gave Clinton $675,000 for three speeches in 2013, and Morgan Stanley, which paid her $225,000 for one speech the same year, both spent millions lobbying the U.S. during Clinton's term at the State Department.

Nearly three dozen of Clinton's benefactors spent more than $1 million annually on contacts with officials and Congress during the same year they paid her to appear at their corporate or association events, according to federal lobbying records. Many earned millions more in government contracts—indications of the regulatory and policy stances the groups might advocate during a Clinton presidency.

General Electric, which paid her $225,000 for a speech in Boca Raton, Florida, in January 2014, has the most extensive government portfolio. GE has spent between $15.1 million and $39.2 million annually on lobbying. The company has won nearly $50 million in government work since 2008, including $1.7 million from the State Department for lab equipment and data processing during Clinton's tenure. The firm also lobbied the State Department all four years under Clinton on issues including trade and Iran sanctions.

As secretary of state, Clinton visited a GE aviation facility in Singapore and touted the State Department's role aiding GE industrial and military deals abroad. Clinton met with GE Chairman Jeffrey Immelt once about the agency's efforts to salvage a planned business exposition in Shanghai and also talked with him by phone ...

4. Foreign countries and defense contractors that have donated to Clinton or her foundation received significant weapons deals during her tenure at the State Department

From the **International Business Times:**

Under Clinton's leadership, the State Department approved $165 billion worth of commercial arms sales to 20 nations whose governments have given money to the Clinton Foundation, according to an IBTimes analysis of State Department and foundation data. That figure—derived from the three full fiscal years of Clinton's term as Secretary of State (from October 2010 to September 2012)—represented nearly double the value of American arms sales made to the those countries and approved by the State Department during the same period of President George W. Bush's second term.

The Clinton-led State Department also authorized $151 billion of separate Pentagon-brokered deals for 16 of the countries that donated to the Clinton Foundation, resulting in a 143 percent increase in completed sales to those nations over the same time frame during the Bush administration. These extra sales were part of a broad increase in American military exports that accompanied Obama's arrival in the White House. The 143 percent increase in U.S. arms sales to Clinton Foundation donors compares to an 80 percent increase in such sales to all countries over the same time period.

American defense contractors also donated to the Clinton Foundation while Hillary Clinton was secretary of state and in some cases made personal payments to Bill Clinton for speaking engagements. Such firms and their subsidiaries were listed as contractors in $163 billion worth of Pentagon-negotiated deals that were authorized by the Clinton State Department between 2009 and 2012.

The State Department formally approved these arms sales even as many of the deals enhanced the military power of countries ruled by authoritarian regimes whose human rights abuses had been criticized by the department. Algeria, Saudi Arabia, Kuwait, the United Arab Emirates, Oman and Qatar all donated to the Clinton Foundation and also gained State Department clearance to buy caches of American-made weapons even as the department singled them out for a range of alleged ills, from corruption to restrictions on civil liberties to violent crackdowns against political opponents.

As secretary of state, Hillary Clinton also accused some of these countries of failing to marshal a serious and sustained campaign to confront terrorism. In a December 2009 State Department cable published by **Wikileaks**, Clinton complained of "an ongoing challenge to persuade Saudi officials to treat terrorist financing emanating from Saudi Arabia as a strategic priority." She declared that "Qatar's overall level of CT cooperation with the U.S. is considered the worst in the region." She said the Kuwaiti government was "less inclined to take action against Kuwait-based financiers and facilitators plotting attacks." She noted that "UAE-based donors have provided financial support to a variety of terrorist groups." All of these countries donated to the Clinton Foundation and received increased weapons export authorizations from the Clinton-run State Department.

5. Clinton put a wholly unqualified donor and superdelegate on a nuclear policy board with access to top secret information because he thought it would be cool. Her staff at the State Department even mocked his lack of qualifications in email.

From ABC News:

Newly released State Department emails help reveal how a major Clinton Foundation donor was placed on a sensitive government intelligence advisory board even though he had no obvious experience in the field, a decision that appeared to baffle the department's professional staff.

The emails further reveal how, after inquiries from ABC News, the Clinton staff sought to "protect the name" of the Secretary, "stall" the ABC News reporter and ultimately accept the resignation of the donor just two days later.

Copies of dozens of internal emails were provided to ABC News by the conservative political group Citizens United, which obtained them under the Freedom of Information Act after more the two years of litigation with the government.

A prolific fundraiser for Democratic candidates and contributor to the Clinton Foundation, who later traveled with Bill Clinton on a trip to Africa, Rajiv K Fernando's only known qualification for a seat on the International Security Advisory Board (ISAB) was his technological know-how. The Chicago securities trader, who specialized in electronic investing, sat alongside an august collection of nuclear scientists, former cabinet secretaries and members of Congress to advise Hillary Clinton on the use of tactical nuclear weapons and on other crucial arms control issue

Fernando's lack of any known background in nuclear security caught the attention of several board members, and when ABC News first contacted the State Department in August 2011 seeking a copy of his resume, the emails show that confusion ensued among the career government officials who work with the advisory panel.

"I have spoken to [State Department official and ISAB Executive Director Richard Hartman] privately, and it appears there is much more to this story that we're unaware of," wrote Jamie Mannina, the press aide who fielded the ABC News request. "We must protect the Secretary's and Under Secretary's name, as well as the integrity of the Board. I think it's important to get down to the bottom of this before there's any response."

From **McClatchy DC:**

A top aide to then Secretary of State Hillary Clinton appeared to mock the appointment of a major Democratic donor with little experience to a sensitive government intelligence board allowing him the highest levels of top secret access …

"Couldn't he have landed a spot on the President's Physical Fitness Council?" Deputy Assistant Secretary of State Philippe Reines wrote in a State Department email in 2012 to two other Clinton aides.

Multiple investigations regarding emails, donations, possible money laundering and now a criminal lawsuit for two of the four men murdered in Benghazi are ongoing and critical.

Hillary may be one of the first women nominated for the Presidency, but she is also the only candidate for that high office who is running while under criminal and civil investigation.

The Hillary Clinton is cracking, but needs much more work to get to the meat of her corruption. The mainstream press, always a liberal supporter, does not do its job as a pillar for the people.

America is in trouble. We don't need a liar, a money launderer, a sick woman with a Marxist agenda to lead us back to prosperity, strength and peace.

You decide.

www.ingramcontent.com/pod-product-compliance
Lightning Source LLC
Chambersburg PA
CBHW050754290526
45792CB00008B/2180